MW01222952

A Plot of Light

by

Susan McCaslin

OOLICHAN BOOKS
LANTZVILLE, BRITISH COLUMBIA, CANADA
2004

National Library of Canada Cataloguing in Publication
McCaslin, Susan, 1947-

        A plot of light / Susan McCaslin.

Poems.
ISBN 0-88982-197-6
I. Title.
PS8575.C43P56 2004   C811'.54   ·   C2004-900992-3

The Canada Council | Le Conseil des Arts
for the Arts | du Canada

We gratefully acknowledge the support of the Canada Council for the Arts for our publishing program.

BRITISH
COLUMBIA
ARTS COUNCIL
Supported by the Province of British Columbia

Grateful acknowledgement is also made to the BC Ministry of Tourism, Small Business and Culture for their financial support.

Canada

We acknowledge the financial support of the Government of Canada through the Book Publishing Industry Development Program for our publishing activities.

Published by
Oolichan Books
P.O. Box 10, Lantzville
British Columbia, Canada
V0R 2H0

Printed in Canada

for Olga

Contrary to what has been thought in recent centuries in the west, the spiritual or interior life is not an exclusively private affair...

The spiritual life of one person is simply the life of all manifesting itself in him.

—Thomas Merton
from his Introduction to
Gandhi on Non-Violence

Contents

A Breviary Of Visions

Transcultural Poetics

Contemplation in a World of Busyness

Main Street Elegies

A Breviary Of Visions

Thereafter the day shall come
When I will pour out my spirit on all people;
Your sons and daughters shall prophesy,
Your old men shall dream dreams
And your young men see visions.

—Joel: 2.28

JOY

She is Wisdom, my lost child
self, my daughter with sky eyes.

She is Sophia. I am still giving birth
to myself as she gives birth to me.

She is Blake's Joy. She is
unplumbed starfire. She is

breathing. Yes. She is.
We are singing to each other.

The wet child is slipping between
our thighs like a white dolphin.

Star-thrown.

SUN GOLD

God appears and God is light
To those poor souls who dwell in night,
But does a human form display
To those who dwell in realms of day.
                    —William Blake

Crux of everything,
why should I not be devotee

consecrating all that flows
from your mere touch

your fragrant word?
Tongue-tied then and now

I track the old ravines,
stumble in the gullies and ditches

losing and finding myself
a thousand times

in your luminescence.
Human, human God

who dwells in light,
dwell also in my dark.

LACRIMAE RERUM

The tearfulness of things
has entered my bones.

Why? I cannot recall.
Some heartbreak or other.

Many times since
in times of greater heartbreak

no tears at all. These not-tears
are virgins' lamps,

hot oils anointing starry sky,
cleansing everything.

Nothing remains sullied
in their wake.

Like breakers they soothe
the crisscrossed shore.

BOOKISHNESS BANISHED

Book bag woman
nose in book

in the grocery line up
or on the toilet

after making love
or with a flashlight, tenting.

Fiction, biography,
classics or trash,

print rolls my head around.
I read in my sleep.

Words, my profession,
words, my accusers

and champions.
Word-haunted woman

word heated and chilled.
Itinerate wordsmith's

open shop and season.
Zen feats of mindful

eating and reading.
Libraries relax me

more than boudoirs.
Secrets on vellum.

Heart is a hand press.
Letters set me dancing.

Alphabets fall from my ears
as from God in the beginning.

I am crazed with codes.
No wonder my Maker

is a silent word.
No wonder this opening

behind purple drapery
is to sumptuous silence.

NAMED, UNNAMED

First you draw me by my name,
then unname me.

I am under your name as one
nameless.

Yet such tenderness in the calling
of a name.

Anyone so named
can never be completely

lost, having been paid
the utmost attention

as a satin leaf kissed
before leaving the ash

or a beloved dog
before quitting its skin

beside a highway.
Form, skin, essence

all named, loved,
every uncountable

nameless hair
named in the Name—

as trillium under *trefoil*
as Madonna lily under *candor*

as the name falling away
under the name rearing its head.

JUST AN ORDINARY WOMAN

One morning a white lamb
is placed in an ordinary woman's womb,

so petite, so delicate
no one notices.

So it might have been
with Mary,

sensing the black hooves
pricking the lining of her womb.

But I am no virgin.
Nevertheless, it is the creature's time,

who pushes against the walls
of a garden grown too small.

She slips out easily, the white one.
Still, the binding cord holds.

My scissors are blunted;
hands fall back on sheets.

The strand unravels of itself
and the lamb rolls over alive

her eyes hurtling into mine.
Sun licks her clean.

How will I protect
such a secret offspring?

What fold will enfold
such fragile power?

PILGRIMAGE

No resting.
The pilgrim hovers over herself

on the steep ascent,
part of her climbing,

part still floundering
on the slippery slopes

of the tarns below
in a maze of malls

in a consumer frenzy.
She has left behind her name

but wants some key to reorientation.
The orient man in saffron

has implicated her
in an intricate plot of light.

Coming up to a halfway house
neither here nor there

she pleads for directives.
If you really desire the kingdom come,

he says, *love this dark sod;*
then kisses ground zero

where wild goldenrod nod
in a cloud of lit mist.

BEAUTY AND BANS

It is clear there has been an earthquake
and everything is breaking up.

The edifice that might have held munitions
or ironworks looks like cracked glass.

Maybe it's an educational institute
housing professors in madcap gowns,

a bank or administrative tower.
Weighty business goes on inside

and the atmosphere is muggy.
I am not afraid to have such brawny escorts,

tough guys like stevedores
just doing a job they've done before.

They are getting me out before the thing collapses.
Why does my head tingle?

Why do I feel like gulping big globes of air
and wobble a little crazily on my feet?

FACELESS BENEDICTION

The faceless bearer of the benediction
is not austere despite the dark gown.

It is someone friendly, someone known
from childhood's round.

The blessing lingers.

It perfumes the day
making silence not a thing to court

but something one is inside
like a snail in its coil

or mountain in its thick cloud.
The hands pressing down

spell more than alphabets,
more than personal consolations.

What they say rings the body,
circles of sound moving out.

IN THE CAVES OF THE SEA LIONS

Brown flesh hunkers down on sleek rock face.
Would that the world could sustain

such lolling about, such disdain
for ledgers, accounts.

Though, diving for the occasional fish,
they accomplish more than those

who stare at their concentrated abandon.
Big Daddy shoves Junior into the deep

in play or territorial dispute.
Behind a grid with all these strangers

shuttled down an elevator shaft
from the highway to the damp sea air,

how can I wed such work or play?
One cow throws back her head and sirens

an arc of bellowing praise.
Bulls' stentorian riffs recur

cooking up a blast, cacophonies
for a polluted coastline.

Some ghostly, aquiline companion,
witnessing everything through my eyes

infuses nothing but this one desire:
to be just a moment outside the glass bowl

letting my unwieldy land-lubber bulk
slide off the rock and grow flippers

serpentining through the underwaves
like a gravid ballerina in her element.

CROSSWISE

Blast of vision,
who can describe a living cross?

Who would believe that pieces of you
like shards of stained glass

have melted into my bloodstream?
A river falling uphill,

a reversing waterfall.
Somehow when you entered your own

utmost poverty, time flipped.
Pileated woodpecker's crimson

and energetic tapping is your knock.
The voice that burns from everywhere

and nowhere, opens all frames.
Each day the mirror gives back

another crease, a fold, yet I am new.
Each day a little death, a downy quilt

or comforter kicked off.
Each sorrow, furrow

brings me nearer where you are
to rise and fall again,

dear Androgyne,
who leaves me trembling here.

A CYLINDER OF LIGHT

Like a swirling tube of blue light
like a milk bath in the head
like suddenly being lighter
like being inside a pipe organ
like light improvising
like a gentle cooing of doves
like a natural hot spring
like resting in energy
like something else doing the work
like pulsations with pinions

like
like

ANTON

a friend who died in a car crash, 1968

You wear blue, your favourite colour.
Your acne has cleared.

You have the same wild laugh,
same way of talking with your hands.

You are not the body gored.
You are not ghastly or ghostly.

You have a body
and tell ribald jokes.

This meeting is a privilege
and we know it,

though it is not timed.
Your love of history

and law keeps you curious
about then and now,

and you still write poetry,
no longer struggling

for the air that kept you here,
no longer trying quite so hard

to arrive at where you are.

NIGHT OF ECSTASY

Who dares speak of a ravishment
so far from *rape* one needs new words?

Origen originated the discourse,
patristic commentary on the *Song of Songs*.

Bernard, Catherine, Teresa, help me now!
This rush is not deserved or undeserved.

Nothing in one's practice brings it on.
Such derangement, showering blisses.

Am I out of myself, ecstatic in kisses,
or inside Another? Who cares?

All categories and classifications fold
when Presence fills the spaces of the soul.

Love loves, speaks Love,
all loves and all is well.

This touching is and is not of the flesh
we bathe and wrap and mutilate.

That body anguishes out of its grief
into places of unnoticed joy.

Whatever comes afterward from this spiral,
the soft delicacy of touch

arches our ordinary steps across time
and recollects itself, singing, "O, my Désirée."

PHAEDRUS

You do not understand this revealing.
Years and years will pass

Before you have the faintest perception
of its significance.

Nevertheless, you must hold on to it.
Your service is a descent. Starts high

when you are young, then plummets
down into things. So how could you know?

Hunched over a computer screen,
shoulders again seared by sensation.

Three fingers strain
to rub the ticklish shoulder bumps.

Drenched like cabbage leaves in dew,
invisible pleated skin erupts sheer

wings too tender for defence.
The Avian Lord soars somewhere in the ether,

while the cunning serpent of the Nile
dreams of flight.

EVERY SPACE ENFOLDS SPACE

Our cameras and probes reveal nothing
but craters and ice-grey rock—

but crevasses of the brain breed worlds.
Women of the moon, for instance,

dance flamenco on billows of aqua ice
and men are artisans in silver.

Barter is usually fair and leisure long.
The place is not utopia though.

Two quarrel over a price
while one talks of how fear

sometimes muzzles people's dreams.
Folks die and mourn their dead.

Yet nowhere did this traveler see
soldiers dropping bombs and bread

over an impoverished country;
Nowhere did some dine sumptuously

while others a short way off served in rags.
Either the technologies of mass destruction

had not yet been invented, or the swords
had been beaten into ploughshares years before.

LOVE YOUR ENEMIES

What if the dreamer surrendered herself
to the scary man in the bear costume?

The children might escape,
leaving the man beating his fists on the ground.

What kind of evil does he portend?
Rape? Murder? Systemic violence?

He is not a person or a country.
His dance of hatred and rage

strips and steals the skins of animals
to disguise a bottomless fear.

Of what is he afraid?
Children's spontaneous laughter,

toothless gums at the breast,
a future that does not know his name?

Perhaps his own emptiness, if he halts the offence.
The dreamer stands stock still on shore

imagining both her certain extermination
and the strange thing love might do

to change the weary, inarticulate
bulk of him, or loosen the knots of his heart,

should she take him in her arms.

A NEW EARTH

Ideology wears khaki and hoists a sub-machine gun.
It is not the end of the world,

just the comfort zone we have known
with its millionaires and malls of merchandise.

The landmine-scarred earth
groans in her sleep, expelling these intrusions

like fibrous epidermal growths
soon to be sloughed off.

She is so beautiful in her sleeping,
sea moss hair fallen in green strands

over capacious stony arms.
Sludge and detritus stain

her broken, camouflaged flesh.
Nuzzled by a vagrant white-tailed deer

who lays his rack of antlers at her feet,
she rolls over into her estuary,

falls down her canyon breaking into mist.
Inside her bones, her hands, her feet

new cells extol the virgin in the crone.
A soft aubade accompanies her rebirth.

Relief maps burn, their corners turning up
to expose a fresh geography of desire.

THE PRAYERS OF THE ANIMALS

The notion of some infinitely gentle
Infinitely suffering thing.
              —T.S. Eliot (from *Preludes*)

The kingdom of heaven is a lens
to wide-open turquoise eyes,

sea-quarried saucers of the black
and white lions who are unselfish.

The purest and most beautiful one
is hard driven over a cliff.

His bones are broken again;
flanks flayed in everyone.

The mushroom cloud is not a prediction
but the fear from which we hide our faces.

The truth is, such lions cannot be killed.
Let's suppose many small animal helpers,

real animals of many species and tribes,
breathe the breath of life

into the wounded heap that is the lion's bones.
Suppose for an instant

we are indebted to the prayer of Fox
with his bushy tail on red alert,

or Mink, with her winsome peering,
and that even the warrior Hawks,

whose pitiless minds are darkened,
are caught off guard (for a moment)

by some infinitely gentle,
infinitely suffering thing

resounding in their hearts,
dissipating the Armageddon cloud.

CLOWN OF GOD

Right in the middle of mid-life,
Christ the stand-up comic

trades my resolute grimness
for laughs—

turfs my bag of tears
and makes it sail

clean across the stage of my life,
as if I wouldn't miss those complex

blocks, those outgrown psychic
toys—as if I never needed them.

Once ousted by such a trick,
never to return? Ha!

Forgiven seventy times seven,
they march back legion.

Big, small, packaged differently now—
humility keepers.

So I am learning like a fool to spin,
toss, juggle—that old expertise of clowns.

FUGITIVE POEMS

Where do the fugitive poems go
when they have escaped our lines?

Do they lie frozen like sperm
in some celestial bank account

waiting to fertilize the imagination
of someone more deserving?

Or perhaps they samba to jazz
orchestrations of our abandoned desires.

They present their backs, slim prints of feet
as when Moses surveyed God's backside.

Sometimes we get the glint of them, the gist.
Perhaps it is the poems

still circulating in our dreams
that keep us tuned

to some unutterable, undelineable
beauty, laming us, making us weep.

DANCING WITH MY BLACK MOTHER

The darkness in her broad face
sequesters slavery's sorrows

as if drawn straight up from Egypt's land
packed like a bowl of sugar

sweet, soft, and dark.
Black Madonna, rock me home

to azure heaven.

Your locket unlocks a tale
of the white man's breath,

the stark hotel
that called you "wife."

And the wee one
who came forth squalling

in the sequined night.
Mother of black pearls,

fragrant bodice,
large working hands,

wheel me endlessly
into the cloud of your dark,

circle my marked face.

LET YOUR YES BE YES

How often the idiot debater
gets a toehold!

Pros and cons,
If this . . . then that . . .

Reasons good and bad
contend in the Cartesian head.

Or Rodin's thinker
bends the body

to a hunched will.
Eyes on ground,

ruminations abound.
But clear-eyed intuition

is a girl who knows what's what,
strolling right out of the store

into the bright day of her yes
that could be a blue velvet coat,

or something else—
a solitary trance among the pines,

the circle of a poem's breath.
A love affair with blue for blind eyes.

DREAM CABLES

for my spiritual mentor, Olga Park, who died in 1985

Who tore down the cables
so none of mine got through?

How could I forget her living voice?
She taught me to play chords

as a master pianist presses
hands over a student's on the keys.

And the squeaky discord
she called music.

In the humility of beginnings,
she assumed proficiency would come,

showing, "letting go into silence"—
the boomerang of grace,

God in the dimmed violet,
God in the sunflower.

All the rooms that spill from her house
as the cottage rebuilds itself

through cords and pinions of prayer
are warmed by her syllables sounding the air.

A TAPESTRY OF FRAGMENTS

for Olga Park

One day it comes: the big commission
for which one is totally inadequate.

Once the master Jesus came to her
saying, "Will you do this for me?

When she replied that she couldn't possibly,
He said, "Never mind, I will perform it."

So such things get done
but the doer does nothing

except to sit and wait
and watch the lovely fragments

of tapestry fall into patterns
as when the spirited vermilion leaves

of the Fall vine maples
wed the cast off rags of the plum.

Today I am sewing some pieces
of her broad but secret life,

the sweep of it, the grandeur
no one knows or will know.

But when I find myself
among the arc of students

on the floor, or rising from my seat
to speak, the words are a chapter

of an older story, a piece
of a cloth woven before my birth.

Those who are not good with their hands,
may be weavers of words.

Seen from the back
the threads seem loosened and askew.

What do I need to know about the view
when the pattern is spread out whole?

Transcultural Poetics

THIRTEEN SONGS ON A MERTON PILGRIMAGE

1. ROCKIES, PRAIRIES, TUNDRA*

Soaring in the silver belly of a plane
over BC's coastal mountains

anxiety lifts, burdens of control
momentarily laid down.

Leaving what you've made—
a prerequisite of birth.

Ground below, and up here
in the silence

these words:
You cannot fly outside the mercy.

* *Poems written during a pilgrimage to Prades, France, the
birthplace of religious writer, social activist, poet, artist,
photographer, pioneer of east-west interfaith dialogue,
Thomas Merton.*

2. MOTHER'S DAY

Frail elder in white booties,
my mother, blissfully inattentive
to her own most simple needs
lies under the blanketing mercy.

New blood from the transfusions
circumnavigates her veins.
Pumped with the haemoglobin of others,
she triumphs briefly over death

while her firstborn, cushioned by clouds,
frets endlessly,
endlessly short of the mark,
recalling how from a bottomless confusion

the mother spoke her daughter's name
in a flicker of cognizance—strand
by which the two of them hang
as from a single branch.

3. PILGRIMAGE

Extracting myself from a maze of my making
demands a three-day navigation chart—

lists laid on fridge and desk,
reminders of lessons, homework, appointments,

all so my own dim arrangements
might fall into the mid-spring lap of France.

Secretly the broad sun sails behind clouds
and my little craft also, beyond my wiles.

Heavens, I am homed in a half-known tongue
with companionable bread-breakers

each clasping a scallop shell
of sorrow beyond my knowing.

My world of lists and orderings sails
or fails without me.

The boon of this journey?
Sweet inconsequence

of all these trials,
my little note sounding

alongside the croon of blue
pigeons in an ivied wall—

mockingbird's sweet song.

4. A DESCENT INTO PRADES

birthplace of Thomas Merton

A friend last night in a dream,
wearing his most uncomplicated face,

spread before me a white sheet—
musical tablature

notation of swirls and swells
unhitched from time.

If I could re-enter
the oceanic cadence of his voice

through the scales of my body
I would know for once

how even my most obdurate reef
cannot withstand

the rush and swell of love—

5. ST. ANTONIN NOBLE VAL

Southern France, where Merton attended grammar school

Round stone cheeses on brown tables,
pink marble tiles against white Pyrenees.

The roofs of St. Antonin are snails' backs
coiled red and cream

along Medieval streets
only a cart can manage.

Here young Tom confronted the bullies,
plucked from the tarn his photographer's eye.

6. ON CONTEMPLATION

Better not to define it.
Every moment brings new seeds.

Call it a long loving look at the Real—
an eremetic gaze at Mt Canigou.

Symposium of seekers,
wayfarers gathered in this room

with a Presence that dismisses nothing.

Rounding tired selves in its arms,
it lounges comfortably on the back step.

Poetry dwells too in generous dark
awaiting the one

who will press into her forehead
a fine blue flame.

7. HOMESICK

Hindu-Pakistani conflict threatens
a festival of nuclear rain.

I would be home with my loved ones
but find myself wandering la Rambla

in Barcelona, where buskers
do the Michael Jackson moon dance

and gaudy clowns cup their hats for change.
The buxom señora dragging bucket and mop,

head bound in blue kerchief,
hovers in a courtyard

of wrought-iron balconies
staring over vendors and touristas.

I have dropped my bustle and haste
while she takes up hers.

8. THE FACES OF LIVING THINGS ARE ALL ALIKE*

The elegant French lady's face, carved reredos,
the German teen's face, sadly efficient,
the English, American, Canadian faces
more like my own, sharing a common tongue,
the Spanish taxi driver's face, ivory against a dark cloud,
the amiable faces of the street dogs in Prades,
the swirled faces of scarlet poppies alongside a road,
the wide, arresting face of the albino gorilla in the
Barcelona zoo,
the cautious faces of two Muslim men
sporting American flag t-shirts in the airport lounge,
the pursed face of the uneasy millionaire,
the bland face of the street snail
poking up out of its intricate staircase of shell.

Faces of stars in the kingdom's blind corner.

*Black Elk

9. HAGIOGRAPHY

At the Thomas Merton conference in Prades,
after a week of speculation
on the life and writings of the spiritual master
who was born here at the foot of the Pyrenees
in the sign of the Waterbearer,
one Israeli woman pronounces,

"Merton, Schmerton! I'm getting tired
of hearing about Thomas Merton."

Maybe the mischievous monk would be
tired of his own personality too.
Would he have married the nurse M.,
run away to Latin America or Alaska,
or returned to Gethsemani, Kentucky
after his Asian pilgrimage when the reclining stone
Buddhas' emptiness and compassion
broke open his brow?

"Keep the fire watch for your time,"
I hear him say,
"Who am I to publicize this emptiness?"

10. THE NIGHT HAS VALUES THAT THE DAY NEVER DREAMED OF*

Night—
    a black river doing yoga

the chickadee's robe of sleep
    the wide ribs of stars

heaven's tablature disguised
    song's fall out of language

into a deeper musicality.

*Thomas Merton

11. JESUS SAID

"You are all divine sons and daughters,
like me,"

so we made him God Almighty
resplendent in vacuum.

We, the incarnation,
blazing

will not imparadise ourselves
by shattering the world's necklace of atoms.

Even so, the gate within us swings open—
small, forgotten inner space.

12. MISSING HOME

No girl-woman with whom to dissolve in giggles.
A continent and an ocean
between me and my husband of twenty-three years.

Wistfulness.

13. ON MY MOTHER'S EIGHTY-FIRST BIRTHDAY

Be with my mother, Gracious Presence.
Tell her of the pinwheel-eyed dogs of Prades—
though she is beyond such telling—
how they stroll at noon on rose-quartz pavements,
defecating freely in La Place, unleashed, unashamed,
and of their fond, exploratory snouts,
their fair, large ears,
their careful attentions to tourists.

Tell her of the little yellow train
that ambles through the Pyrenees,
and of the waiter Claude who dances the tango
at Hotel Les Glycines, hotel of the hyacinths,
and of the rapt roses blistering in roadside stands
and of the stunted peach trees scoring the hills.

Sprawl alongside her, Spirit, on her bed.
Where her paper-thin flesh is torn, make a small mend,
and when she is tickled by some incommunicable joke
and laughs to herself
tell her in your wordless way
how I know she has forgiven all my faults.
Tell her that even the mangy dogs
are entering into paradise by the scruffs of their necks,
that God in us, stricken, exiled,
groans and travails in her most inarticulate ramblings.

Be with us now and at the hour,
O merciful Companion,

Infinite Patience at the heart.

Contemplation in a World of Busyness

QUEENSWOOD

1. SURRENDER

Entering this precinct under the icon of St. Anne, an angel places a card in my hand containing the single word—*surrender*. I surrender to the hospitality of these nuns for five unstructured days. What must be surrendered? All the matrix of home chores and organization. I surrender barges of books. I surrender motherliness, laundry, dishes, homework *en francais*, wifely support. I lay down punctuality, lawn care, home economics, hearth-goddess, dog walking, emails, meetings of the Board, brainstorming. Disarmed, someone with my name falls wondrously down into the dark, hyacinth-scented, loamy nest prepared for me in my Mother's house.

2. IN MY MOTHER'S HOUSE ARE MANY MANSIONS

In my Mother's house
        (drinking blackcurrant tea with lemon)
I am a work-in-progress
        (folding back pages and scribing marginalia)
Having an into-the-body experience
        (by peach brick walls)
From Ex-stasis to In-stasis
        (soft as flesh)
Climbing from the womb on a ladder of bones
        (grammar of laughter)
What embedded worry-cross
        (right in the middle of her forehead)
Uncrosses itself on the first night
        (even though she was horrid)
Brown moth by the poolside
        (folding back lanced wings)
Completes its karma and dies
        (object of silken attention).
A deer has walked the labyrinth before me
        (dear deer)
Remembering the goddesses in the tale
        (sharing one eye among them)
She is glad for her one eye
        (watching it pass from hand to hand).

3. FINDING THE FATHER IN THE MOTHER'S HOUSE

Amo, ergo sum.
                    —Simone Weil

This blood-remembering is hard
harder than the earlier time of touch and speak
time of dawdling in your blue Buick
in the elbow of English Bay
where we talked obliquely of your imminent death
time of redress, time of the profusion
of tears by a rectangular grave
harder than the flag-draped coffin

and last days spent avoiding
the indignity of hallways
frustratingly skinny limbs
crooked arms that could not close
on a daughter's last embrace
with nothing left to control or fix
nothing to do but remember as I do now
unsaid words, shuttle coach
that blazed you straight
across the stars while I slept,
deaf dust, in a net of domestic care.

Now I walk a coiling labyrinth
past browning hydrangeas
late blooming fuchsia
to its center where you wait.

I imagine what words you will say
and how I shall answer them.

4. MIGRATING INTO GOD

Time to lose the habitual motions—
from the flicking of the switch
to the thoughtless word.

Time to do a stint at release,
to unclasp clasping
as when peridot beads

slide from the neck
and white arms fall
from the prison of their hold.

Time to set the heart afloat
in the wide grey strait
with the wild island geese.

5. BUILDING THE SPIRITUAL BODY

Not like a leaky apartment, board by board,
but more like a secret doorway of the brain,
as when Kepler first imagined Neptune
burning in its gaseous haze.

So what was always present
floats at last into our domain,
like the vagrant planets
with their blue and orange moons,
red spots on Jupiter,
brewing a continual storm.

6. CERES

Looking back over my life, the best moment of all was when I gave birth to my daughter, first gazed into her luminous, azure eyes. This surpasses everything else, and there is no way to describe it. I loved her tenderly and cared for her with great gentleness. Now that she is poised between girl and woman, I love her no less. May she go forth, irreducible, unrepeatable, into her flourishing. Whatever losses, sorrows lie along the way, I cannot see, but my heart knows she will overcome all obstacles. May the power of Sophia, the great Mother, accompany her, and be with her in the hour, should she give birth to another.

TRANSFIGURATION

Someone leads you up a mountain,
tabors chiming in the air.
Eagle Mountain or Burke,
Golden Ears cocked to heaven.

Day for seeing, letting the glance
pause along a sinuous ridge
where spires cut sharp into cumulous.
Day for breath, expansion.

Let's say that backpacker guide,
your long-time friend, should turn,
commenting on the distance remaining,
and meet your eyes with such flame

you think him someone other than himself
for just a moment, someone so dear,
so wise, he could beat away the coming dark
with his hands, yet holds them out to you.

You will build no cairn at the summit
to the moment when the careening sky
churned the sleep of your bones;
you will carve no initials in the cliff.

Yet somewhere in that blissful zone,
abyss of dark and bright past words,
you and the friend will dance
phosphorescent, over remembering rocks.

MY TENTH MUSE

Tenth Muse, you climbed an academic tower,
finding me lost in busy solitude,
burnt raw with poems, vestiges of power
stolen from alternate worlds I'd cut and glued—
a propped up ragamuffin house of bark.
Then some mysterious momentum, love,
settled within our floundering, wayward ark
like a small genius lost in larger love
or the steady magnolia on our lawn,
receiving and relinquishing everything.
Our husbandry, a kingdom lost and won,
so nothing is devoid of you in spring;
in winter you're the sacramental meals,
the Poem which my stream of poems feeds.

NO PALINODE

My love for you demands no palinode
since compiled years bring nothing to retract,
our minds at play, our bodies somewhat slowed,
tenderness rocked past certainties we lacked;
yet never any dire uncertainties
over the rightness of the path we carve
despite the wayward twists, grim qualities
of baleful Time, his starvelings in the nerves.
Concatenation of our separate names
made a girl-child from mercy and the hour,
transformed her into will and dust and flames
and set her on a road beyond our power.
O constant Love, alive in all my breath,
be present in the coda of my death.

TENDER INWARD

You save me from the temptation to fly
from metaphor into dry abstraction
connecting me to spiralling songbird's cry
that pierces heaven, nuances every action.
I kiss the tender inward of your hand,
a daybed where skittering shadows dream
your kindness, the abundance of the land,
eagles' consortium by a salmon stream.
To say I know you is true and untrue,
your thoughts and habits, sensible and clear;
yet part of you, while I was sleeping, grew
to boundless amplitudes inside the ear
where the Father in secret uncovers
the oiled hinges, opens doors to lovers.

A LAY TO THE RELAXED
(if there be any such living)

Pardon my quarrel with Tom Merton
the monk, contemplative, activist,
or Bob Lax (lax and loose)
his best friend who ambled
twenty-five years on Patmos
writing minimalist poems

but let either of them trade their ascetic lives
for one whirlwind month of teaching, children,
lawn care, council proposals, editorial assistance,
carpooling, proofs, meals, laundry, renovations
for their eremitic or coenobitic flow,
and just take a few notes.

Let them try to be artists, contemplatives,
mothers, wives, colleagues, board members,
friends, pet owners, tutors, grocery shoppers,
home redecorators, guardians of teenaged chastity,
referees of fights, peacemakers in the home,
sexy consorts in bed, budget managers,
nurses, and friends—
then count the holy breaths.

TO ONE WHO HAS LOST AT LOVE

Be chary.
You are sad
that such a torrent of extravagant love
languishes in the barrels
unsipped.

Who will drink with me this cup?

Think of God
whose rings and jewels, stacked deep in cellars
whose rifts of sound
and amplitude of shocking scarlet vine maple leaves
arrange themselves in a prolix waste on the inlet trail

while all the distracted full go hungry away.

Think
how in this welling, uncertain ground
unknown, untouched, silent

lies the lonely, abandoned Godhead
against whose lavish, unjudging presence
we raise our small fists of resistance.

THE PRACTICE OF WALKING

Man was made for Joy & woe;
And when this we rightly know
Thro' the world we safely go,
Joy & woe woven fine,
A clothing for the Soul divine . . .
             —William Blake, *Auguries of Innocence*

Past the gate, mental projects swarm.
Papers and plans and plots

arrange their tight trajectories,
books and print swirling.

One—the President of Concern:
a family matter involving loss.

Down the lane, lodgepole pines
interrupt this brain chatter.

A bumblebee and a monarch butterfly
visit the same purple-mouthed thistle,

one flirting, one sucking deep.
Pace makes supple the wandering mind.

Suddenly, then,
you are without reason—

outside yourself—
burnt fragrance of Cariboo air

filling the muscles of your thighs,
carrying your dusty veins up and over

the first hill past a second curve of road.
Ochre thought tugs at the knots in your mind.

Three hills later through a poplar grove
two startled grouse, brown and white ruffs,

melt into the salal.

Imperfect, perfect world—two-fold
holding us inside, as we fasten eyes to rim.

Mind intent on the same hard stuff,
peels it down to a white rod, divining

joy and woe in herbicide-bitten foliage.
You enter the enclosure of cabin,

spill words like stains on a page:
Know this—

your life will not be perfect
except as you love

whatever comes
joy and woe woven fine.

Main Street Elegies

In memory of my father, Donald Arthur McCaslin

If the spirit of a man at death saw truly what he was and had been, so that whether he desired it or not a lucid power of intelligence manifested all himself to him—then the energy of that knowledge was especially urgent upon men and women here.
                              —Charles Williams

SPOTS IN TIME

You tell us stories of your childhood in Panama:
how you sat under the teacher's desk
looking up at her massive hairy legs;
how you were jealous of your best friend
and snaffled his piece of birthday cake;
how you defended a kid from his brother
and ended up fighting them both;
how you sliced your foot with a machete
and walked home with a blood-oozing shoe;
how you got lost overnight on Ancon Hill
and had to be rescued by the Marines.

You show us pictures from your high school annual
of you playing clarinet in the band,
a photo of "Donald" stretched out full length
showing off your hand-made remote control model
airplane which still hangs in the rafters
of the rec room.

The story you tell us most often is this:
how at four-years-old you paused
halfway up an ordinary flight of stairs,
and decided to hold in memory forever
this day, this hour, this instant,
this one worn step.

SATURDAY MORNING SUPER-DOOPER-WHING-DING BREAKFAST

Great strips of greasy bacon,
hunks of Jimmy Dean sausage hit the fry pan.
You prod the eggs in leftover fat,
swearing you'll enjoy yourself
before cholesterol coagulates,
blood pressure skyrockets.

Next, you bring on mounds of toast,
laden with butter half an inch thick,
explaining how the habit began in the army
when the troops lacked butter for months.

Then come fried potatoes, grapefruit, prunes,
milk and juice, marmalade, a variety of jams,
all like your Dad made them,
and finally, a jar of peanut butter.

Mom, a vegetarian since she saw a sow
with a tag in its ear at the Puyallup fair,
disdains your fare, but we kids
devour the succulent feast.

FALLING

The falling begins at work.
I get a call that you have gone over
without warning like a giant cedar,
crashing across filing cabinets,
gashing your lip, head.

At home you topple
on the way back from the mailbox,
shatter your hip
just as my husband and I leave for Europe.
I phone from Dublin and your voice
tries to sound normal, cheering.

The doctors diagnose Lou Gehrig's disease,
the same that felled your uncle Don.

Over the phone again
you call this your "death sentence."
I flail on black ice—
the finality of words.

PASSION

Before you become totally unable
to control your body, you tell me
this slow death, coupled with no real
diminution of consciousness
is a worse torture than Christ's on the cross—
his lasted hours, yours, years.

I want only to console, to enter your state:

Christ crucified in you,
yet living on.

PROGENY

Eight years into my marriage,
when you are dying,
I carry one-month old Claire Iris
into the room where you lie
helpless, tended by my brother.

You have always believed
you would survive through your progeny.

Now, a month after Claire dances into time,
I lay her on your chest—milky offering—
breathing into life, as you breathe
your departing.

OLD NEWS

Father, I see you
clasped in sleep,
curled child-like, restive,
gaunt shoulders heaved
through fugitive, foetal dreams,
tangled weirs where sons
and daughters turn away.

This news is old—
a man dies alone,
goes somewhere,
wrapped in vagaries.

"It isn't death I mind
or the naming of death,
but the passage through—
arms, legs, useless,
heaving for breath."

Brain fretted with fire rants,
"I will." Skull open
to the awe-ful real
whispers, "I cannot."
Cannot go, cannot
move again
with elegance
through time.

DIS-EASE

Father, in your slow war
against muscles' atrophy—
sleeping nerves disengaged
from vital wires,

flight of sinew and flesh
from healthy bone—
I watch and wait and hope
for prayer's effectual balm.

An engineer, you stare
at death's derangement,
trying to break it down,
but it defies you,

till you imagine sod
falling from clattering shovels,
salting your white bones.

"It is a lie," I want to shout.
The mind in death does not suffer
body's embarrassments; divested
of flesh the soul flies free.

Sometimes I see Death—
an opaque wall turning
clear as glass as you
pass lightly through.

PRISM

You are fighting against decline
but call to relate a waking dream:

a prism held aloft—
colours twirling and twirling in the light.

GRATITUDE

From the hour the doctor delivered the news
you never evaded or denied death,
never sought miraculous cures, divine intervention,
but watched the disease progress—
unflinching soldier.

You joked about how to reach death
without bankruptcy, fearing the costs
of being a terminal patient.

The last time I saw you
you said you were climbing
an endless hill, unable to crest the ridge.

OUT ON A LIMB

You creep out on a tree's finger,
covet a sequined sky:
"I want, I want."

You glide with the mallard
till the stream narrows
and you breathe "the end"

but the end is the tip
of a hawthorn wand
and from it flows light

surprised at the second
wind that blows free
from a samite cave.

Leaden, soldiering through
sodden fields,
you dream of flight,

hitch a ride on a loon's back
and, arms wide open,

shout your name
into the heart of the galaxy.

ELEGIAC

I weep, but the elegy has not begun.
Its music enters months after your funeral.

Driving to work, I hear your voice
saying my name, triggered
by a popular song you liked,
filling the air.

DREAM

Before you die you tell me this dream:

you found yourself
hurtling across space to the other side
of the universe, fearless, exhilarated—
an exploratory flight.

What pavilions did you build here
that rose to meet you there?

To what did your dark night open?

PRESENCE

Sometimes when our daughter is acting out
of her imagination—
questioning, laughing,
I sense you a little to one side.

How do the dead surround us?
In love—through love—by love.

ELEGY

My daughter came, my father went away
within the circle of a single year—
one joy, one grief, held in two seasons' sway.

The biting loss not tempered, but held at bay.
When death's the summit, who can conquer fear?
When my daughter came, my father went away.

For everyone who toils, one comes to play.
Upon the viper's nest, the innocent's tear.
One joy, one grief held in two seasons' sway.

I bind my grief in rhyme to make it fray
like cloth that unravels and is sere
while daughter comes, and father flies away.

This death, this life, merge in a single way
by which we come and go and learn to bear
one joy, one grief, held in two seasons' sway.

From one bright light rebounds a two-fold ray.
My daughter, come, my father, pass away—
one joy, one grief held in two season's sway.

LEAP IN THE DARK

When you made the great leap into Being,
my brother said your eyes
were fixed on something unseen—

you plunged inward, fully conscious,
gulping air and light.

Saying *no* to the machines,
you chose to die

as you chose
the *yes* of your birth.

Acknowledgements

I wish to thank Hiro Boga at Oolichan Books for her helpful editorial advice and the loan of her musical ear.

"Bookishness Banished" and "Dream Cables" have been published in *Room of One's Own*, Vol. 25, No. 4. Selections from "Main Street Elegies" appeared previously in *Bellowing Ark* and *West Coast Review* (now *West Coast Line*). "A Descent into Prades" and "Pilgrimage" appeared in the *International Thomas Merton Society Quarterly News*. "Joy," "Lacrimae Rerum," "Just an Ordinary Woman," "Crosswise," "Night of Ecstasy," "Phaedrus," "Dancing with My Black Mother," and "Let Your Yes Be Yes," have been published in *The Journal of Feminist Studies in Religion* (Harvard Divinity School). "The Practice of Walking" appeared in the anthology *Poetry and Spiritual Practice* (The St. Thomas Poetry Series), and in *Prism International*. "Anton" was published in *Kaleidoscope*. "A Descent into Prades" and "Pilgrimage" appeared in *The Quarterly News of the Thomas Merton Society of Canada*.

About Susan McCaslin

Susan McCaslin is a poet and Instructor of English at Douglas College in Coquitlam, B.C. She is the author of nine volumes of poetry, including *At the Mercy Seat*, *Flying Wounded*, *The Altering Eye* and *Common Longing*, and the editor of the anthologies *A Matter of Spirit: Recovery of the Sacred in Contemporary Canadian Poetry* and *Poetry and Spiritual Practice: Selections from Contemporary Canadian Poets*. She lives in Langley, B.C. with her husband and daughter.